Images of the Mountain West

in Photographs and Poems

Images of the Mountain West
in Photographs and Poems

Beth and Don Paulson

Twain Publishers
Chicago

Twain Publishers, Lake Point Tower, Suite 5306, 505 N. Lake Shore Drive, Chicago, Illinois 60611-3410
leroux@twainassociates.com

Printed in USA

ISBN: 978-0-578-50462-9

Also available from Twain Publishers:

Paulson, Don, 2015. *Mines, Miners and Much More*.
Nelson, Kent, 2016. *Rescues and Tragedies in the San Juan Mountains*.

Introduction

The Mountain West is a vast part of our country, replete with richly varied scenery. From the high peaks of the Rocky Mountains to deep canyons, wide plains, and deserts, it can be said to encompass eight states.

Inland sea, ice, volcanic shifts, water and wind have shaped this land over geologic time. Where native people lived first, much later Spanish explorers, trappers, miners and ranchers worked in and settled. Today the region's national parks, monuments, and wilderness areas attract great numbers of visitors as communities and government agencies cope with decisions about how best to preserve its open and wild places.

For over four decades we have travelled in and then made our home in southwestern Colorado near Utah and not far from New Mexico and Arizona. By jeep or in hiking boots, we have experienced close-up the grandeur and beauty of these lands. Our adventures together in many sometimes remote and always unique places have inspired us to take hundreds of photos and to fill journals with poems.

From breath-taking summits of Colorado "Fourteeners" to the heart-stopping waters of the Colorado River we have shared high moments. We have journeyed through plains and deserts, marveling at the emptiness of spaces, as well as beside fields and pastures of historic ranch lands. In forests from piñon and juniper to wind-bent spruce we have walked dozens of trails. And we have looked closely at great numbers of wild plants and flowers, letting their names live in our mouths, paintbrush to potentilla.

In this book we offer to others, in our images and words, some of the places and experiences we have been inspired to treasure.

Beth and Don Paulson

Receive

Wildflower Basin

When one blue columbine
opens for you and shows you
raindrops on white and blue petals,
bows slightly in wind that blows
across the valley between the peaks,

how can you see the whole
meadow of other wildflowers
shaking out their carpet of color--
yellow daisies and pink fireweed,
bushes of bluebells, and a
rainbow of paintbrush?

It's too much for the bees, too--
they buzz drunken,
heady with happiness, and
tiger-striped butterflies leap and loop
from flowers to waterfalls
all day in the sun, short-lived,
tireless.

Tumbling Down

Before a waterfall in early summer
      you stand in awe. How the river
drops precipitously so fast, so powerfully
      over the sheer lip of smooth rock
plunging into a turbulence of air
      scattering so much white light.

      You don't want to leave but kneel.
        Breathe deep the cooler air
      into your parched body, feel its mist
        on your upturned face,
      on new-green grass, unpocket your griefs.

      When Li Po visited the waterfall
        on Mount Lu, he wrote he saw
      violet smoke rise and the river waters flying,
        that he dreamed the Milky Way
      had tumbled down from heaven.

Li Po (701-762) was a Chinese poet of the Tang Dynasty.

Little Red Elephants

After golden-eyed ducks
  have hatched in the shallow waters
of high mountain meadows or streams,
  look for elephants' heads
spiking up from deep-green ferny leaves.

Purply-pink, exuberant, they
  flourish in beaver ponds and bogs.
If you look close at a bloom
  you will see one tiny lip
is an ear, one is a trunk.

Count yourself lucky when you
  come upon these in the wild:
there are no other flowers
  like them in the Rockies!

Green Hearts

New leaves are spiking outside my kitchen window,
pale, delicate, unfurling from a bare aspen like tiny scrolls.

Underneath it long fingers of iris have pushed up
from bulbs hiding in the moist mystery of earth.

Another sign, yesterday I saw yellow forsythia
sprung out from a tangle of branches in the garden.

At the sink I stand in awe, no words for these gifts,
I who have also felt the broken will of the body,

been lost in the dark, uncertain alleys of the mind.
Even in my unsteady hand, when I hold up

this clean glass to a beam of light, it reflects back
through the window an offering of green hearts.

On Mount Elbert

Sun's just past sky center on this perch of graveled earth,
end point of a long morning my muscles surmounted gravity
to get me up so high where wind and sunlight magnify.
I sit, breathe deep, laugh, stretch weary arms and legs,
down shoulders ease my pack into a shallow shelter

other hikers built with boulders, then pocket for a young child
one small stone. Far down I mark the path of my ascent
past tree line, bowls of sapphire lakes, thin ribbons
of gray road, then circle my body in 360 views, reach out
with my fingertips into this clarity of blue, farthest
I've ever hiked up where the rest of Colorado slides away.

Marmot

No wonder we see you
rusty furred and bushy-tailed
on the top of a boulder
sunning yourself
on a late August morning
halfway up Mount Sherman--
you spend 4/5 of your life
in a underground burrow,
much of it in hibernation.

No wonder we see you scurry,
fill your grizzled muzzle with grass,
then tumble down a well-worn path
to a doorway under rock
to stash these winter stores.

No wonder you whistle-chirped
as we came up the trail
to warn your offspring,
then sat very still so we might
suppose you were the boulder.

No wonder on this snow-free
summer day I am in envy of
your agility and tenacity,
as I reach out with bare hands
and bent legs, crab-crawling up
a steep talus slope.

En Plein Air

High up in Imogene Pass in late July, a meadow
is spread over with rosy paintbrush
all the way from jeep road to snowfield edge.

If Monet came here, he would sit all day
in his broad hat before his easel trying to
capture on canvas this spread-out carpet of color
fed by snowmelt, woven beneath a tundra slope.

He would mix madder, vermilion, a bit of white
to try for the particular shade of clustered bracts,
little dabs of color he would apply to the canvas
he carried up from Telluride. Maybe he would
also sketch hummingbirds and bees as they
sipped and hovered in the sweet-scented blooms.

When light changed over the San Juans, his quick
strokes would catch the movement of late-day
winds that wash like waves across the wide meadow.

Back home he would smile telling his friend Pissarro
their American name and how it felt to breathe thin air.
He would say at 12,000 feet how near he felt to heaven.

Pond Study

Sat down by a quiet pond
glassy green in noonday sun

breathed in water-heavy air
saw ripples form and disappear

by cattails, reeds, and mossy grass
drifted snags by willow banks

where dragonfly and damselfly hovered
then darted in sun-lit arcs.

Touched where water striders skimmed
shadows, silver minnows flitted

gazed at floating water boatmen
snails on bottom rocks, algae, silt.

Sat down by a quiet pond to rest
but all was busy-ness

from beneath the wavy mud
to what teemed from extravagant depth.

Larkspur

I first see them
by a mountain lake,
profuse along
the shore we walk.

Majestic, royal,
those blue blooms,
little star clusters
on each green stalk.

A rock for my seat,
I rest for a while
in wonderment,
in a galaxy, wild.

September Yellow

In the yellow season
rabbit brush grows profuse
and pungent at the roadsides,

bouquets of golden eye daisies
reach skyward. Tall sunflowers
lean, black-centered and many-

branched against the rail fences.
On the hillsides aspen
leaves change to gold,

their light flickering in blue air,
like moths or small flames.
This is a time of dying.

You know that means
you and I will die, too—
perhaps with slow aging or

a more certain diminishment
or we could be struck in sunlight
sudden as the eagle in flight

seizes the heart of its prey.
I want to believe there's no grief
in this, but a gratitude.

October Fire

Evening not yet
evening,
the sky burns blue
behind the hills
and if you wait
awhile on the
unpaved road
where you
stop your car,
you will see
the blue catch fire
turning the sky
ochre, then orange,
then red, beyond the
bones of trees,
black roof of a barn
and you might
feel the darkening
earth beneath
holding you
in the solid
planes of its shadows
even as it spins
and journeys
in faith,
in constancy.

Winter Trees

Ice-dazzled, trailside trees
        gleam,
each branch altered to white
        overnight.

                Explainers says it's
                        atmospheric--
                river fog and cold collide
                        to rare display--

                                while others see in these
                                        frosted winter trees
                                under early morning sky,
                                        glitter-light, mystery.

Recall

Even a Desert Thirsts

Out of our canyon camp we hiked all morning
in wet boots, meager gear, upward on a sandstone path,
slick from steady rain. Shivering in its chill,
we stepped across gullies, streams running red with silt.

Distant thunder groaned, lightning sparked bruised sky.
We shifted packs, talked little. Once I opened my mouth and
tasted rust in the rain's sweetness. You named plants we touched,
bent from wind and water: *brittle brush, black brush, salt brush.*

There were green willows in a seep we stopped to rest, rock-sprung.
Even a desert thirsts. That afternoon when the dark clouds passed,
we lay down on the sun-warmed rock and gazed over our heads
to a shining tower of vermilion sheltering us, time-worn, immense.

Slot Canyon

Ancient waters scoured
these crevices and spirals
in red sandstone I climb
bending my soft body
to fit unyielding curves.

I trust my feet to grip,
arm muscles to pull me
to each higher place.
If I fall, how far?

Where space opens up
wide enough for two,
you grasp and clamber first,
hold your strong hands to help me,
find us shallow footholds,
sunlight assuring exit
from this labyrinth.

How will we be changed
when we finally emerge to blue
sky and juniper desert?
Will the world?

Mesa Arch

Consider how we arrived by jeep
to an island in the sky,
walked a path down through
claret cup and Utah juniper
on an early summer day high
heat had not yet reached.

Consider how this arch came to be
out of an inland sea, vast, primordial.
How salt-spill, sand, rock debris,
birthed dome to ridge to fin
until ice-crack, wind, and flood
wore it away to what we see today.

How its delineaments astonished us:
an eye-slit to clouds, blue sky,
doorway to white-rimmed desert,
window to the snow-capped La Sals.

How it felt to sit and rest for a time
in its penumbra, cool our hands
on blood-red and umber rock, feeling
with them its smoothness, its declivities.

Consider that even now this singular door
is open to let in the winds, the rains,
that time here is but a memory of water.

Stone Creek Woman

Canyon wren trills
    down a stone staircase.

Black raven skims
    across a rock rampart.

In the heat of mid-day
    the desert dazzles you.

When at last you lie down
    in the cave pool of a falls

you see Stone Creek Woman
    limned in wet sandstone

her veil cool water,
    her hair velvet moss.

At the Great Gallery

We catch breath when we finally see
      those armored giants, great panoply
to wonder at. Who painted them
      two thousand years ago or more
           and why high on an alcove's stone?

God, man or shaman wears the crown
      with armless body, shield-like shape
painted blood-red on lighter rock,
      mystery of designs incised,
           marching with others in a line.

We share the language water knows
      beneath these tall red sandstone walls
where we take in sage-scented air,
      shelter from the noonday sun
           in a grove of cottonwoods.

Remote museum or place of bones
      long gone to dust? What words were said
or sung, sacred or quotidian?
      Whose whispers on the wind?

Only the hidden canyon knows,
      its sheer swirled sides carved eons deep
where new footsteps mark streambed damp
      along curves of sand and shallow seep.

Balcony House, 32 Steps

Take hold of a ladder hewn of strong timber
worn smooth by many hands, and grip with yours
one rung at a time. Lift legs, plant boots
firmly under you, with each step breathe deep.
What matters here is sun and moon.

When you reach a ledge wide enough to rest,
cool your body in whistling wind, listen for
ancient drums in a circle of pit-become-kiva,
sense sage smoke, songs of weavers, hunters,
low notes of wild turkeys, rhythmic grinding of
metates, shouts of a bare-skinned boy to his dog.

At the Mountain Top

Up here I can almost
touch the changing clouds,
taste the dust of the earth
on my lips, dirt that rests
at day's end in the lines
of my rough hands.

On this steep side of one
high mountain, work is hard,
but the pay is good,
five dollars a day and
three hearty meals.

Mornings it's down the shaft
to the level for *mi compagno*
and me. At the face it's cool
in summer but loud with
hammers and drills.

At shift end when we step
out of the hoist, how bright
is the sky over our heads,
light that lasts so long after
la cena, we play cards.

And from my window
at night in the bunkroom
I cannot count all the stars.
Yet Colorado is so far away
from la mia madre patria.

All Aboard!

Here where narrow gauge tracks
round a hill, the 2-8-2 engine chugs
upgrade through forest and field
on a sunny summer day
rail fans and families love.

When the tender takes on water
at the tank, steam hisses.
At a crossing in the valley
three loud whistles sound.

120 years ago mountain lines
grew towns like Chama, NM,
Durango and Ridgway CO, places
a man could work his whole life--
engine to roundhouse to section shed--
for pay enough to keep a family.

You could order from Sears Roebuck
and get your goods at the depot,
travel across the country if you had
money for a ticket, take the train
to Denver to buy a winter coat.

Today a passenger in a bill cap leans
his camera out a window at the curve
to photograph the engine, the smoke
uncurling overhead, to capture the past
in the present. Listen. You can still
hear its echoes down canyon.

County Road

fence leans
ditch runs
dust blows
weeds grow

grass bends
trees sway
leaves fly
rocks crunch

clouds scud
peaks shade
winds shift
truck hums

birds soar
crows caw
horse trots
dog barks

boots step
arms swing
sun heats
heart beats

Autumn Psalm

Praise the bright landscape
of green field and blue sky.

Praise the quieter creek,
ice-edged on cold mornings.

Praise great rolls of hay,
red-roofed barns and fences.

Praise snow on the mountains,
black cows with white faces.

Praise yellow school buses,
their drivers and children.

Praise chimneys and woodpiles
on porches of houses.

Praise all who live in them.
Praise anticipation.

Ghosts

Beside the road
a ranch house stands,
unpainted, summers
nearly hid by trees.
On one side it's shaded
by a leaning spruce
that's grown taller
than its sloped roof.

The family gone now
or moved away,
others feed cattle,
mend fences, mow hay.

Can you see
the front porch,
hear a swing creak,
a couple's low voices,
children in the tall grass
playing statues and
hide and seek?

Snow Day

Sunwarmed, we unzip
Gore-tex jackets
stopping our skis'
climb and glide, catch
breath, small clouds
in the blue air, sip water
from aluminum bottles.

In a San Juan winter
a hundred years ago
each day was a snow day
for young men who came
from far away to work
for adventure and good wages
in these high mines.

In worn hobnail boots
they hiked uphill mornings
from their boardinghouse
through new-fallen snow
to the hoist house
for a day's labor
where gold and silver
hid deep underground
in hard rock tunnels.

On this day all is silent
save for soft wind blowing
through the tall firs and pines,
their voices long gone
with the ringing sounds
of their hammers and drills
that once echoed
through the white hills.

Reflect

Reflect

to turn back or throw back
as a rock wall reflects heat
on a warm day;

to give back an image
or likeness as water
reflects the steep slopes
of a mountain;

Is the pond blue or
is that the hue of the sky
it reflects?

to think carefully, meditate,
ponder, deliberate;

Do not be the person
who reflects overlong
on the end of the journey
before she sets out
on the upward path.

Wild

One ordinary day
if you are lucky
you may come
face-to-face with
utterly wild beauty.

You first hear a
soft step in dry grass,
snap of a tree branch
before you glance up
and a deer emerges
from a nearby woods,
stands perfectly still,
and lets you look long
at its muscled body,
its fur the color of
the forest floor,
its antlers, gold velvet.

For one moment
you gaze into
the dark pools
that are its eyes.
For one moment
you both know
no fear, joined
in the immensity.

The Bighorns

For a month a herd of mountain sheep has lived
in the grassy field north of the cemetery

on Highway 550. Light brown, almost
silvery, these stocky, muscular

bachelors stand or sit close together
in the sun. Their full-curled horns nearly touch.

Drivers slow down, stop in the pullout
to capture them by phone or camera,

these thick-necked bovids, white-rumped
and muzzled, as they graze and ruminate.

Each time I drive by them I think
they might have already taken their leave

for the higher country before summer,
where, hiking, I once glimpsed a small herd

silhouetted above me on a rocky ridge.
One framed me in his sights,

lesser, backpacked creature on two booted feet,
slow climbing in his terrain, deep breathing his air.

Ice Lakes

I dreamed I walked between two lakes,
circled by mountains and endless sky.

Below me long and grassy steeps
fell into a basin of willow brakes.

When we reached the first blue lake
(or was it a fragment of summer sky?)

I held onto a narrow path,
my feet climbed over fallen scree

hands gripped outcrops of tumbled rock.
The higher second lake was green

with an knobby island of brown earth
out in the middle that some of us

swam to, the water brisk and deep.
On the way back down to trees and road,

rocks, flowers and lakes stayed behind--
only the wide sky followed me.

Gentians

Along a high meadow path
       above the firs and pines
past white rocks
       some big as miners' cabins

the mountain gentians
       unfurl five pointed petals
of such deep blue
       the ink maker only dreams.

Bend your face into their slim leaves
       amid the wild grasses and
you see some keep tight closed, waiting
       for mid-day sun.

If you return by the same lucky path
       the gentians spill open their blue bottles
as when the poet Li Po dipped his brush,
       earth and sky joined.

Canyon Notes

How to understand *river*:
ride eight days on its back
between walls time carved a mile deep
rose blood-red gray-green black--
not yet speaking its language
give it words
swift-running silt-laden shimmering.

Mornings wake to mud-colored riffles
where current surge and splash
wet shirts to flesh shivers--
afternoons dream in still places
skin hot in sweaty drowse

until dusk shades the river platinum
its rush muffled by cool sand
where pink tamarisk grow
like feathers among boulders
and sacred datura open
diaphanous as moths
where at night moonlight rides
on ripples cast with uncountable stars.

Light Can Be Both Particle and Wave

A small bit, so small
as to barely be seen;
part of something larger;
part of a whole;
from the Latin particular;
A particle of dust
in a shaft of sunlight.

A minute portion of matter;
an object with mass
but without size;
subatomic particle;
proton, neutron, or electron;
elementary particle;
lepton, muon, Higgs boson.

A particle acts like a wave,
a wave like a particle.
I am made of particles
of water and salt;
my body moves in waves.

An object existing in a dualism
between the continuous
and the discontinuous.

A particle has being and motion;
a particle is real;
it is a theory.
It is all things;
it is no one thing.

A particle is only part of the truth.

Land That Moves Back and Forth

Ten miles out we watched cloud shadows
sweep across dun-colored hills
transformed to massive dunes
back-dropped by Sangre de Christos
over 14,000 feet, snow-capped in October.
Closer still the mounds lengthened,
unmetamorphic expanse stretched north
to south, a changing, ancient horizon.

Water, sand, wind--we only need three words.
You reach out your hand to pull me
when we slow-climb the closest one,
higher, deeper as air swirls, sands sting,
form waves we ride to the summit,
squint at behind sunglasses
before gravity pulls us like moonwalkers.

All day time's construct expands.
I hold breath to meet it, watch
afternoon light spill, shadows shift
over dune faces, sands shape to fold, hollow, slope.
Perdonanos nuestros pecados tambien.
Forgive us also our trespasses.

By night we've grown spare, our need only
to shelter in fragrant sage under *alimosas.*
Hours slow. Awareness swells.
Ripple to bar, drift to ridge,
sand has already erased our footprints.

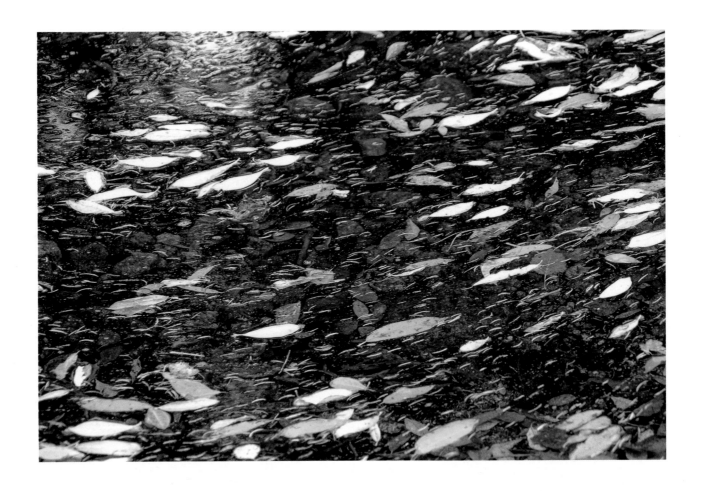

By the Creek

Up in the Rocky Mountain Park
I hiked beside a pool.
It was a late October day
and against my face and bare hands
a cold wind blew.

It cast down leaves across the path--
some floated in the pool
and stilled there for a little time.
So thin they lay atop the water--
what beauty to behold.
A few had gone to gossamer,
a few were beaten gold.

Mountain Grandeur

Late light resting on the curve
of a red mountain transforms
to sunset. What it leaves behind:
a dark ridge, morning's snow
dusk-blue on the north faces,
in the shadowed meadow,
snow like spring flowers.

You hear something flicker,
whisper in the tall, pointed trees,
but it is only the body of the wind
moving past you to cast ripples
on a small pond where
a second sun rests, shimmers.

Behind you, such beauty,
ahead of you, only memories
of this day, of this moment.

Aubade

Why is the sun so slow so far away,
sky gun-metal over the hills
where winter will soon empty the trees,
snow fill them up again,
the earth behaving as if nothing were wrong?

I am trying to love what lives
a little longer—
all the yellow leaves that whirl
and fall to the ground with no regret,
bright berries of mountain ash
each one a little sun.

Winter Willows

Along ditch line and creek bank
      water barely flowing
or in vacant frozen snowfields
      the willows turn vermilion.

      Beside the snow-packed highway
          they're a bright profusion
      tangled, curled and whip-like
          brazen branches, shining.

            When the shroud of winter
              holds the dead land tight,
            blazing with presumption,
              they cast amazing light.

Renew

Fir Tree

Make me like the fir tree
draped in falling snow.

Keep me rooted
to the needled earth

through drought and storm.
Give me supple branches

to bend with heaviness,
with uncertain winds.

Make me generous as the fir tree
that offers a mountain home

to finch and grouse,
shades the summer hiker,

shelters the silent deer.
Let me also be content

with my place in this world.
Make me like the fir tree.

Chop Wood, Carry Water

I have become a winter field,
      vacant place covered with snow
      where silent fog grazes.

I have become the black bones of trees,
      white drifts along the road
      the wind whispers across.

Edge of a river hung with ice,
      blue shadow of a pine,
      lean filigree of willows.

I have become the empty space
      between words,
      outline of a mountain peak,
      sketched gestures of deer.

I have become the woman
      whose footprints make a path
      to the woodpile, the frozen well.

The more I become still,
      the more I am able to hear.

Epiphany

In spring wind
three horses play
in a new-green field,
manes blown back
like open sails.

So intent they are
in their pleasure:
no stasis but
a wild epiphany
in your blood rises
as in theirs.

Pasqueflower

Sometimes you must wait for one thing
      that will change your life.
Whoever reaches the limits of longing?

Yet the world is made again
      each morning the black silk of night
         shakes and the stars fall away
and the fire tongues of the sun
      announce field and tree and mountain.

And one day the cupped bud
      of the white pasqueflower
         spreads its silvery filaments
out of a bed of new-green leaves
      and, like a small fist,
         out of damp earth, rises.

In Beauty All Day Long May I Walk

May I greet every morning with a song of gratitude.

May sunlight that kindles the land warm my heart.

May the words I speak bring peace to the people.

May I walk lively on the paths set before me.

May an eagle carry me on its wings when I falter.

May earth embrace my spirit in my departing.

Title is taken from the Navajo Way Blessing Ceremony.

Claret Cup

One of your names is the color
        of wine, little cups
for a king, but you are also
        scarlet, ruby, carmine.

How you astonish summer,
        burst forth in rocky outcrops,
desert and mountain dweller,
        echinocereus of three spines.

Navajo *amá sánis* once gathered
        your flowers, stems to make
sweet cakes, your fruit to concoct
        a medicine for slow hearts.

Today I take with me the memory
        of your blooms for love, desire,
and when I need them, rage and courage,
        blood-red as fire.

Compass Flowers

Above tree line
on steep grassy slopes
sprung from scattered rocks

grandiflora flourish untended,
bright yellow sun goddesses
all turning east

their full-petalled faces.
They are not versed
in the ways of the world

but in them sun lives.
Compass flowers
called by early surveyors

crossing difficult terrain
to tame and map a nation.
They survive still, flourish

between clear blue
and cloud, between snow
field and high mountain,

all a-tremble, unfurling
until the wind turns
its back and they fold

into their secret deaths.
Not at all boastful
how they raise, bow

their golden heads
every day of summer
and not one is disregarded.

Camp Robber

If you want to meet
the gray jay,
take a picnic lunch
up into a high forest.
You might hear its call first --
hoot-hoot tch, tch, tch--
or just see it swoop in
from a pine branch
and steal a bite
of your sandwich.

This bold bandit's
a mischievous creature,
a camp and cabin pilferer,
downward winging master
of the snatch and grab
who lines its nest with
feathers and fur
and lives for free.

Aquilegia Elegantula

I am dreaming
    of red lanterns

in a Japanese courtyard.
    Rain is falling softly

on the tile roofs.
    A young woman plays

her lute and sings
    a sad song about

the lover she left behind
    in her village.

She wears a red silk kimono.
    Her face is pale,

her long hair held up
    by ivory combs.

The flames in them flicker
    gold in the night wind.

Something Radiant in Our Lives

When I was walking
    where the aspen trees grow,

wind began to shift the heart-shaped
    leaves. They tossed all-trembling.

Or was it water moving pebbles
    in the shallow creek?

I kept awhile beneath them,
    stood close to one where

speckled light entered its gnarled eye.
    I touched its papery bandages.

Then the wind blew harder
    and a hundred bright coins

spilled out from the purse of the blue sky.
    I knelt down in the wet

fragrant earth and gathered up
    a handful of gold.

Even When I Cannot See

This morning fog has lain
a shawl over the valley,

mist-knit, breeze-borne.
How it holds the green fields

of white-faced cows in their purpose
of slow-walking, grazing the grass.

How their large black bodies
gleam, dew-coated and regal.

I, who share breath with all creatures,
pause a moment in this beauty.

Even when I cannot see
where there is to get to,

I am held in the weightless embrace
of cloud, of air, of stillness.

Nightfall

Luminance crosses
ridge to ridge,
the sky purples
as light flames
the heavy clouds.

Leaves, flowers
are lost now,
the river hidden
in silky darkness.
Everything that is
not sky blackens.

As shadows flee,
all the long day's
thoughts settle.
Hearts quicken
at this fleeting
brilliance,
then turn inward.

Notes

The photos in this book were taken using several cameras and lenses: a Nikon D70S DSLR with a Sigma 18-200 lens (N1), A Nikon D5200 DSLR with a Sigma 18-200 lens (N2), a Nikon D5200 DSLR with a Sigma 18-300 lens (N3), a Canon SD/1100 (C), an Olympus 4100Z (O) and an I-phone 6s (I). The page number and approximate location for each photo is indicated below along with the camera used to photograph it.

Acknowledgements

The authors would like to thank their publisher, Paul LeRoux, and former Buckskin Booksellers owner Robert Stoufer for their encouragement and assistance in the preparation of this book.

Grateful acknowledgments are also made to the following publications in which these poems first appeared:

Aurorean: "Winter Willows"
Clover: "Compass Flowers"
Earth's Daughters: "Chop Wood, Carry Water"
Eleventh Muse: "Canyon Notes," Second Prize, 30th Anniversary Edition
Grand Valley Magazine: "Ice Lakes"
Innisfree: "Aubade"
Kerf: "Gentians"
Leaping Clear: "Green Hearts"
Mountain Gazette: "Wildflower Basin"
Naugatuck River Review: "Land That Moves Back and Forth," Semi-Finalist, 2019 Issue
Poetry for the Spirit: "Consider," "Pasqueflower"
Ruah: "September Yellow"

Beth Paulson has been widely published over the last fifteen years in well over a hundred national literary journals and anthologies. Her poems have been four times nominated for Pushcart Prizes as well as Best of the Net. She has also been awarded prizes from West Side Books, Mesa State Festival, Mark Fischer Poetry Prize, *Cloudbank*, *The Eleventh Muse*, *Passager*, and the *Naugatuck River Review*. Her poetry has appeared in *Crazy Woman Creek: Women Rewrite the American West* (Houghton Mifflin, 2004), *What Wildness is This: Women Write About the Southwest* (University of Texas Press, 2007), *What's Nature Got To Do With Me?* (Native West Press, 2011), and *Going Down Grand: Poems from the Canyon* (Lithic Press, 2015). Beth's most recent book is *Immensity* (Kelsay Books, 2016). Her four previous collections are *The Truth About Thunder* (Ponderosa Press, 2001), *The Company of Trees* (Ponderosa Press, 2004), *Wild Raspberries* (Plain View Press, 2009), and *Canyon Notes* (Mount Sneffels Press, 2012). She taught English at California State University, Los Angeles for over 20 years. She currently lives in Ouray County, Colorado where she leads Poetica, a workshop for area writers, and co-directs the Open Bard Poetry Series. In 2019 Beth was named Ouray County's first Poet Laureate.

Don Paulson has studied with noted Colorado photographer John Fielder. He has had three solo shows of his photos and won a number of prizes at juried art shows. His photos have been published in several southwestern Colorado tourist brochures as well the Colorado AAA *EnCompass Magazine*. Don is the curator of the Ouray County Historical Society as well as a board member of both the Ridgway Railroad Museum and the Trust for Land Restoration. During the last two decades he has written numerous magazine articles and given talks on southwestern Colorado history. In 2003 Don re-instituted the *Ouray County Historical Society Journal*, last published in 1984, and since then he has edited an additional four volumes of the *Journal*. He has authored or co-authored three southwestern Colorado history books: *Narrow Gauge Railroading in the San Juan Triangle* (2009*), Mines, Miners, and Much More* (2015), and *Peaks of the Uncompahgre* (2016). In 2016 Don received the Ouray County Outstanding Citizen award. Previously Don was Professor of Chemistry at California State University, Los Angeles for 36 years. Don lives in Ouray County, Colorado and enjoys nature photography, model railroading, hiking, and jeeping in the San Juan Triangle.